YOU & YOUR PUPPY

MARION LANE

© T.F.H. Publications, Inc.

Distributed in the UNITED STATES to the Pet Trade by T.F.H. Publications, Inc., 1 TFH Plaza, Neptune City, NJ 07753; on the Internet at www.tfh.com; in CANADA by Rolf C. Hagen Inc., 3225 Sartelon St., Montreal, Quebec H4R 1E8; Pet Trade by H & L Pet Supplies Inc., 27 Kingston Crescent, Kitchener, Ontario N2B 2T6; in ENGLAND by T.F.H. Publications, PO Box 74, Havant PO9 5TT; in AUSTRALIA AND THE SOUTH PACIFIC by T.F.H. (Australia), Pty. Ltd., Box 149, Brookvale 2100 N.S.W., Australia; in NEW ZEALAND by Brooklands Aquarium Ltd., 5 McGiven Drive, New Plymouth, RD1 New Zealand; in SOUTH AFRICA by Rolf C. Hagen S.A. (PTY.) LTD., P.O. Box 201199, Durban North 4016, South Africa; in JAPAN by T.F.H. Publications. Published by T.F.H. Publications, Inc.
MANUFACTURED IN THE
UNITED STATES OF AMERICA
BY T.F.H. PUBLICATIONS, INC.

CONTENTS

Facing Page: A healthy puppy is the perfect companion. There is no end to all the wonderful experiences you will share.

Photographers: Rhonda Dalton, Isabelle Francais, Mary M. Hall, Chet Jezierski, Linda M. McCarty, Robert Pearcy, Pets by Paulette, Sharron Podleski, Vincent Serbin, E. Moreau-Sipiere, Karen J. Taylor, and Wil de Veer.

No matter what breed you choose, raising a puppy requires responsibility and patience.

SELECTING A HEALTHY PUPPY

A new puppy! What could be more fun? A ball of fluff with oversized feet, all warm, wriggly and snuffly, with equal parts of mischief and affection. Think of all the wonderful things you'll do together. Long walks to explore the neighborhood. Rides in the car, and hikes in the woods. Teaching him or her to play catch and shake hands. He'll go everywhere you go, sleep at the foot of your bed, be your best buddy. It's going to be great! A puppy is nature's perfect playmate—as long as he's healthy.

Certainly most puppies are born healthy, and if they are well cared for throughout their lifetimes they can easily live long lives. On the other hand, almost everyone knows at least one sad case where it seems the new puppy had hardly arrived before the medical problems started. It is imperative to take steps to make sure that your new puppy is healthy. Asking questions, knowing what to look for and having a new puppy promptly checked out by a veterinarian are some things you can do that will help bring peace of mind.

ASK QUESTIONS

Puppies are so irresistible that it's hard to be around them and remain a smart consumer at the same time. Make it easy on yourself by preparing ahead of time a short list of questions to ask your breeder. Ask for the puppy's exact date of birth. Puppies should not be separated from their mother and littermates before the age of seven weeks. If possible, ask to see the mother of the puppy and where the puppies have been kept. Ideally, the mother dog should appear to be healthy and friendly (if not

Be prepared with your concerns and questions before visiting pet shops and breeders. A litter of puppies will often prove too cute to resist!

to you, a stranger, then at least to her owner) and the litter should have been raised in a warm, dry environment, not outdoors, in remote locations, in cold or damp surroundings, or on bare ground. Be wary of any situation where there appears to be more dogs, especially young litters, that can possibly receive individual attention from the breeder, as puppies and dogs need lots of close interaction and attention from humans in order to fit well into their future families.

Ask what kind of veterinary care the litter has received, and request that this be given to you in writing. Typically, new puppies will have received their initial vaccinations at six or eight weeks, and will have been dewormed

Health should be a pressing concern when trying to decide where to buy your puppy. Always ask your breeder to see the litter. If the kennel is clean and the dam and her puppies appear to be in good condition, your puppy has probably received a good start in life.

Question the owner of the puppies about the kind of veterinary care the litter has already received. Have they been given their initial vaccinations? Were the parents screened for genetic defects so that the puppies will be free of hereditary disorders?

(almost all puppies inherit roundworms from their mothers) at about the same time. Also ask what kind of food the puppy has been eating.

If you are buying a purebred puppy of one of the larger breeds, ask the breeder if the dam and sire were x-rayed to make sure they did not have a condition known as hip dysplasia. This is a very common and often crippling orthopedic problem prevalent in dogs that weigh more than 50-60 pounds as adults.

If you are buying your puppy from a pet shop, you will not be able to see the mother of the litter to judge her health and temperament. Nevertheless, you can ask where the puppy was born, bearing in mind that a puppy born locally would not have been subjected to the stress of

extended travel at a tender age. The same questions about veterinary care are appropriate.

Wherever you are acquiring your puppy, be sure to ask for an opportunity to interact with the puppy for at least 10 minutes before you make your decision. This is your opportunity to observe how the puppy looks, moves, acts and reacts. Ask to see the puppy play on the floor or other safe surface, and ask to hold him while you are seated (don't expect a breeder, adoption counselor or shop keeper to allow you to hold a puppy while you are standing, as this puts the puppy at risk of being dropped by inexperienced owners).

KNOW WHAT TO LOOK FOR

You don't have to be an expert on dogs to be able to use your eyes, ears and other common senses in selecting a healthy puppy. Whether you are adopting your puppy at a shelter, picking one from your next door neighbor's litter or buying one from a pet shop or breeder, there are some basic things to check for.

Healthy puppies have clear, bright eyes and clean, slightly moist noses. You should not see signs of upper respiratory infection, which include thick, colored or crusty discharge from the eyes or nose, sneezing or coughing and red, hot, inflamed ears. Dark, crumbling debris inside the ear probably means ear mites. Be wary of a puppy who is shaking or tilting his head, pawing at his eyes or ears, or repeatedly scratching or licking a particular part of his body. Check his skin for flakes and scales, sores, rashes and bare patches. Part the hair and look for fleas on the skin around the base of the tail or in the groin area.

Puppies smell good. It would not be normal to find any strong, offensive odor coming from the skin, the ears, or the mouth. Puppies with a lot of hair on their legs and feet may smell of urine or feces if they are not kept clean or bathed; this is a matter of grooming, not of health.

No matter what kind of coat a puppy has, it should feel clean and soft, with no excessive oiliness or dryness. Puppies should have a nice dense feeling about them when you pick them up. A thin, bony puppy may be underfed and/or malnourished, and you will want to know why. A thin puppy with a pot belly probably has worms. Any lumps, bumps and swellings should be viewed with suspicion. If you are not sure whether certain physical structures are normal, check to see if there is a corresponding structure on the opposite side of the body.

> Never decide on a puppy without having the opportunity to spend some time interacting with him first. This is your chance to get a feel for the personality of the pup, as well as how he will interact with you.

Healthy puppies do not wheeze, sneeze, or cough under normal circumstances, although some do breathe audibly or snore lightly while sleeping. Barking and growling during play is normal; sharp cries when moving or being handled signal pain and should be investigated.

Does the puppy seem to move freely and naturally, even if clumsily? Limping or favoring a limb suggests pain. Also look for hesitation to move or jump and any unnatural gait, such as swinging the hips from side to side or giving a little hop every few paces.

Every puppy is somewhat different from every other, but in general, puppies are curious and outgoing. Ask yourself if the puppy you are considering is active, playful and interested in his surroundings. Does he seem affectionate and trusting of people? A very quiet, still puppy may be ill or in pain, and one that is hanging back, hiding, trembling or growling may be meeting new people for the first time— which is not a good sign. Be wary of the puppy who acts uneasily or openly fearful of the person or persons who have been caring for him.

GET A VETERINARY CHECK UP

Once you choose a puppy you should take him or her to be examined by a veterinar-

ian. If possible, arrange to take the puppy to the veterinarian even before you take him home. In the event there is something terribly wrong, the less time you spend together, the easier it will be to return him to the breeder. When you visit the veterinarian, explain to her or him that you have just purchased your puppy and before you grow too attached, want to make

sure he is in good health. Bring along a fresh stool sample and any records you were given that show what vaccinations or other treatments the puppy has received. Expect the veterinarian to perform a thorough physical examination and watch the puppy walk. He will check the stool for parasites,

and if he finds any signs of illness, probably will want to run a series of blood tests to examine the functioning of various internal organs and systems.

Reputable sources will not knowingly offer sick puppies for sale or adoption. On the other hand, most situations where large groups of puppies are offered to the public are stressful, and a basically healthy animal may come down with a minor infection or other temporary condition. Oftentimes, the additional stress of moving into your home may be what causes the puppy to come down with the sniffles or a little stomach upset. These minor ailments usually are easily treatable, and if they occur within a short time of the puppy's arrival at your home, the cost of treatment may be the responsibility of the person who sold the puppy to you.

Unfortunately, other problems may be more serious and/or difficult to cure. These include a number of contagious illnesses that puppies can contract from one another, some of which may be fatal within a period of a few days or weeks. Most of these can be prevented by vaccination and by isolating very young puppies from other animals.

> **Puppies are all individuals. However, a generally healthy puppy will be curious, outgoing, active, and playful. You owe it to yourself as well as the puppy to make sure that he is as healthy as possible before you bring him into your home.**

Once you choose a puppy, make arrangements to bring him to the veterinarian before you bring him home. The vet's examination should be thorough and rule out the possibilities of any illness or parasitic infestation.

A different kind of problem that a puppy may have that may be impossible to detect until he or she is older, is an inherited, or genetic, defect. Defects can range from minor disorders, such as crooked or missing teeth, to major disorders, such as abnormal joints, bleeding disorders and defective heart valves. Unfortunately the only protection against genetic defects is to obtain a puppy from the best source possible. A reputable breeder who will know the puppy's heritage. He or she can almost guarantee that your puppy will be free from these disorders.

some effort to compensate a person for a sick puppy. While you may receive a refund, a replacement puppy, or reimbursement of your veterinary expenses (up to the cost of the puppy), these laws do little to compensate for the disappointment and heartache that you may suffer. Another thing you can do to protect your interests, if not your emotions, is to ask the seller of the puppy for a written contract that will allow you to recoup your loss if the puppy she sells you turns out to be sick.

Perhaps the most important thing you can do is educate yourself about puppies and dogs in order to eliminate from consideration any types that seem more likely to have potential problems. Beyond that, you can do your very best to make sure that whichever puppy you take home receives the very best that you can provide in lifelong care.

Many common ailments that may make your puppy ill can be treated easily and will pose no threat to you or your family.

What can you do to protect yourself in the event your puppy does turn out to be sick? For one thing, over a dozen states now have "puppy lemon laws" on their statutes. These laws require commercial establishments to make

A healthy puppy will be an instant source of love, fun, adventure, and entertainment for your family. He will adjust well to his new environment and quickly become one of the gang!

HOUSETRAINING YOUR PUPPY

Ideally, housetraining should begin the moment you walk in the door with your new puppy. The best way to approach this most important task is to recognize at the outset that a few weeks of intensive effort now will pay off handsomely in many years of living with a dog who can be trusted not to soil in the house.

TRAINING METHODS

Training your puppy where she should eliminate is a two-step process. First you have to show her, in a way that she can understand, what you want her to do. Then, when-ever she does it that way, you have to reward her. This will help impress upon her that good things happen when she performs or behaves in a certain way.

Housetraining methods build on the puppy's basic instinct to eliminate away from her sleeping/eating area. Therefore, what you need to do is confine your untrained puppy to a cozy crate at all times when you cannot actively observe her; this will prevent her from making innocent mistakes all over your house, especially on rugs and carpets where any lingering odor will draw her back again and again. At the same time, however, you must provide your puppy with ample opportunities to relieve herself in an area of your choosing, whether indoors or out. After many repetitions of using her designated area, with enthusiastic praise for doing so, she will learn what is expected of her. Then and only then can you extend the amount of time that she can spend outside her crate, although still within a limited space that can be easily cleaned. When housetraining is complete, your puppy can have free run of your entire home, whether anyone is there or not.

Housetraining will be the first training experience for you and your puppy. Although it may take some patience and hard work now, a well housetrained pup will be a trusted member of the family for years to come.

Allow your puppy ample time outdoors to attend to his needs. Always praise him after he does so.

months, depending on the age of your puppy, her health, whether or not she's already been allowed to develop bad habits, and how consistent you and other family members are in your training efforts.

ADVANCE PREPARATIONS

Plan to be home for several days or, even better, a week or more when you first bring home your puppy. Make sure your puppy is in good health. Puppies with intestinal or urinary tract infections will be difficult to housetrain.

If you haven't already purchased a

There are two methods of training your puppy where she should eliminate: paper-training and housetraining. Paper-training teaches puppies to eliminate on newspapers or other substances laid down indoors for that purpose. It is appropriate for puppies who will not weigh more than about 15 pounds when full grown. Paper-training may also be used temporarily in situations where puppies have not been fully immunized and therefore should not be subjected to the outdoors. Housetraining, on the other hand, teaches puppies never to eliminate in the house. Either way, at the end of the training period, your puppy should clearly understand where she can eliminate and where she can't. The training period can vary from a few weeks to a few

Regular meal times will help your puppy to control her bowel movements, so that she is on an elimination schedule compatible with your lifestyle.

housetraining your puppy

Plan to stay at home for at least the first few days of your puppy's arrival. During this time, your puppy will need your almost constant attention.

To make sure that your puppy thinks of her crate as her own special place, provide her with a comfortable blanket and some toys. Remember never to scold her while she is inside, so that all her associations with it will be pleasant ones.

toward regular, consistent bowel movements.

THE TRAINING SCHEDULE

During housetraining, your puppy's entire day should be divided into time/activity slots and taped up on the refrigerator for easy reference by all family members. After housetraining, it certainly won't hurt to maintain the same basic schedule for feeding and taking your puppy outdoors.

Your puppy's daily schedule should consist of several repeating cycles of these four basic activities: going outdoors or to her papers for about 10 minutes each time; playing and exploring within a limited area for about 20 minutes each time; eating and drinking for about 30 minutes at a time; and being confined in her crate or other small

puppy crate, do so now. Accustom your puppy to her crate by feeding her inside it before beginning her formal housetraining. Never scold your puppy while she is inside her crate or use the crate to punish her. The crate is to be her "den," her very own place of rest and refuge, so all her associations with it should be pleasant ones.

Make sure your puppy is accustomed to being on a leash before you take her outdoors. Feed your puppy a consistent amount of food at the same times each day. Use only high quality food and clean water. Not only is this important to good health, but a premium diet with high quality ingredients is more completely digested by your puppy. This, in turn, helps train your puppy's system

Your puppy's schedule should always include plenty of time for supervised outdoor activity. All puppies need an opportunity to burn off a little steam.

housetraining your puppy

Paper training is an ideal way to housetrain a puppy that will remain small, as well as a convenient method for some living situations.

your puppy according to her age (puppies under three months should eat four times a day, puppies between three and six months three times, and puppies over six months twice a day); be sure to schedule time to eliminate after each meal as well as after waking, playing and being confined. Discuss the schedule with all family members; if several people are going to share in housetraining duties, clearly assign all time slots so that the schedule is rigorously maintained.

Steps

Begin by following the schedule you've set up, but don't hesitate to add or subtract minutes from different activities if it becomes obvious that your individual puppy needs more or less time for certain tasks. Ignore your schedule whenever you see signs that your puppy is ready to eliminate. Typical signs include circling, sniffing the floor, and appearing to be restlessly looking for something.

area that she will not want to soil for 3 or 4 hours at a stretch. Understand that your puppy's natural rhythm will dictate for her to relieve herself after sleeping, after playing, after eating and/or drinking, and after being confined for a length of time. Also note that if you work all day, there will be a period of more than eight hours when your puppy is confined. Clearly this is not the ideal situation, and you are encouraged to try to find a trustworthy neighbor or professional pet sitter who will come in and add an additional cycle to the middle part of the day.

HOW TO PAPER-TRAIN YOUR PUPPY

Materials

• A puppy crate or small confined area that will represent the puppy's den, ideally located in the kitchen or other room where the floor can easily be cleaned, but which is also near the center of family life.

• A baby gate or other barrier to keep your puppy

confined during the times she is allowed to play and explore.

• Standard-size newspapers, stacked about eight sheets high, always in the same location (you may substitute an uncovered litter box and litter if you prefer).

• Enzymatic odor remover, available in pet supply stores.

Schedule

Make up a schedule for

Puppies require some vegetable matter in their diet. The CARROT-BONE™ made by Nylabone®, serves the function of plaque control (mechanical action), appeases your pup's need to chew, and is nutritious. It is highly recommended as a healthy toy for your puppy.

The first few times you take your puppy to her papers, gently hold her there until she uses them; do not distract her by petting or talking. Praise her warmly as she is performing, however, offer only a word or two of mild praise if paper-training is being used temporarily. You do not want to really congratulate your puppy now for something you will not want her to do in a few weeks. Remove soiled papers right away and put down clean ones. Leave one used paper on top to remind your puppy of what she's supposed to do here. After your puppy is promptly using the papers, start calling her to walk to them rather than placing her on them. It's important that she begin to move toward them on her own.

Whenever you catch your puppy making a mistake, in the act of urinating or defecating anywhere except on the papers, startle her by saying "No!" (no need to yell), and immediately take her to the papers. If she finishes there, praise her warmly (again, praise her sparingly if paper-training is only a temporary approach).

Puppies instinctively return to the same areas again and again to eliminate, and their extraordinary sense of smell will easily lead them to the spots. You therefore should thoroughly clean and deodorize any areas where mistakes were made to avoid inadvertently allowing your puppy to be drawn back to them. As your puppy makes fewer and fewer mistakes and finally no mistakes for a week, you can begin to extend her play time until confinement inside her crate or small area is no longer needed. If she relapses, go back a step and maintain for another week the last schedule that allowed her to be successful, then gradually increase her play time again. Only when your puppy has made no mistakes in the kitchen for a week should you begin to allow her into other rooms of the house; even then, observe her closely at first so you can observe and correct any mistakes that she may make.

HOW TO HOUSETRAIN YOUR PUPPY

Materials
• A puppy crate or small confined area that will represent the puppy's den, ideally located in the kitchen or other room where the floor can easily be cleaned, but which is also near the center of family life.

• A baby gate or other barrier to keep your puppy confined during the times she is allowed to play and explore.

• Enzymatic odor remover, available in pet supply stores.

Schedule
Should be the same as described in the above section on paper training.

Steps
Begin by following the schedule you've established, but don't hesitate to add or subtract minutes from different activities if it becomes obvious that your individual puppy needs more or less time for certain ones. Ignore your schedule whenever you see signs that your puppy is ready to eliminate; typical signs include circling, sniffing the floor, and appearing to be restlessly looking for something.

No matter how carefully you select or raise your puppy, accidents will happen. All you can do is be prepared by being armed with a non-toxic, effective stain and odor remover. Photo courtesy of Francodex.

Remember, mistakes in housetraining aren't necessarily your puppy's fault. During training you will need to be very attentive and look for signs that he needs to relieve himself.

housetraining your puppy

It is important during housetraining that your puppy become familiar with his leash. This will allow you to lead him to the appropriate place for elimination.

are pretty sure that she has a need to do so at the time! Do not distract your puppy by petting or talking, but praise her warmly as she begins to perform. Always clean up after your puppy.

During housetraining, you must teach your puppy that the first order of business when she gets outdoors is to eliminate. You can do this by always taking her directly to her bathroom area, gently distracting her from other activities and saying "No!" every time she begins to wander off. Then bring her back to the spot, and as you do so, remind her why she's there by repeating your chosen word or phrase. When she does finally begin to perform, praise her with great enthusiasm. After that, allow her to sniff and explore, meet other puppies and people, and generally enjoy the great outdoors.

Whenever you catch your puppy making a mistake, in the act of urinating or defecating indoors, startle her by saying "No!" and immediately take her to her outdoor area; if she finishes there, praise her warmly. Thoroughly clean and deodorize any indoor areas where mistakes were made to avoid inadvertently allowing your puppy to be drawn back to them.

As your puppy makes fewer and fewer mistakes and finally no mistakes for a week,

When you take your puppy outdoors, always take her to the place you've already decided shall be the bathroom area, and keep walking her back and forth on leash until she eliminates. If your puppy is a male, direct him to appropriate vertical structures that do not include flowers, bushes and shrubs, mailboxes, or anyone's personal property, including automobile tires.

Be prepared with a particular word or phrase (for example, "It's time!" or "Let's do it!") that you will utter as you see the first signs that she's about to perform. Praise her enthusiastically; at time this phrase will become an effective command to your puppy and she will actually eliminate when requested to do so. Obviously you should not make this request unless you

Teach your puppy that the first order of business when he is outdoors is to relieve himself.

you can begin to extend her play time until confinement inside her crate or small area is no longer necessary. If she relapses, go back a step and maintain for another week the last schedule that allowed her to be successful, then gradually increase her play time again.

Only when your puppy has made no mistakes in her enclosed area for a week should you begin to allow her into other rooms of the house; even then, observe her closely at first so you can observe and correct any mistakes that she may make.

SUCCESS?

How do you know when your puppy has been thoroughly housetrained? An entire month of no mistakes while having free run of the house is a pretty good guide. When you reach this point, reward yourself appropriately for keeping calm and being patient with your puppy. You both deserve it!

After your puppy eliminates, allow him time outside to sniff and explore. Puppies are naturally curious and will want to investigate everything that is around them.

Housebreaking can be made easier with pads that are scientifically treated to attract puppies when nature calls. The plastic lining prevents damage to floors and carpets. Photo courtesy of Four Paws.

It is easy to identify a well-fed puppy. An active pup with a shining coat and alert gaze is surely receiving the proper nutrition.

FEEDING YOUR PUPPY

The first commandment of feeding a new puppy is to make no sudden changes in his diet. Abrupt switches in the type or quantity of food, or in water, can bring on stomach upsets. You are advised to find out what kind of food the puppy has been eating. Obtain about a week's supply; then, if you do intend to switch to a different food, make the changeover gradually during the course of the week. Do this by substituting first one-quarter of the new diet and mixing it with the old, then half and half, and so on until you're feeding only the new food. If you pick your puppy up from a breeder, ask for a bottle of the water the puppy is used to, and gradually change over to your water also. However, there are other things to think about in relation to food and feeding.

WHAT KIND OF FOOD?

There are almost too many food choices available to today's dog owner. It can make you think that there is a best or optimum food or combination of foods for your puppy, and that it's your job to figure out what that is. This is not necessarily so. Your puppy will probably do very well on any commercially prepared diet that is specifically formulated for puppies and carries the words "complete and balanced" or "nutritionally complete" on the label. A considerable drawback to commercial diets, however, is that they generally are over-processed, meaning that a lot of the nutrients are lost.

To feed your puppy well, you don't have to buy the most expensive food. Nor do

Never make sudden changes in your puppy's diet. Switches can cause problems from digestive difficulties to finicky eating habits. When making any sort of change, be sure that it takes place gradually.

you have to provide tremendous variety. It's probably not wise to feed one flavor of one brand exclusively, but your puppy will not object to eating the same half-dozen things week in and week out. Try to relax about mealtime. Healthy puppies generally are good eaters unless they are allowed to become picky.

The dog food industry is a multi-billion dollar enterprise in the United States. Commercial diets are classified as generic, name-brand and premium. In general, the quality of diet increases from generic to premium brands.

Generic Dog Foods

Many large supermarket chains offer generic or store brand dog foods for considerably less money than the name brands which may appear on the same shelf. Generic dog foods are considered to be of lower quality than their popular counterparts, and are unlikely to provide optimal nutrition. It goes without saying that a food that does not claim to be complete and balanced almost certainly is not!

Brand Name Dog Foods

These are the canine equivalent of the pre-packaged dinners that you can buy for yourself at the supermarket, which is exactly where you can find the dog foods as well. Recognizable name brands of dog food include Purina, Alpo, Cycle and Ken'l Ration. These brands have been around long enough to have earned a high degree of consumer confidence and are generally of good quality.

Premium Foods

The manufacturers of these diets have gone to extra trouble and expense in preparing their foods, and they cost more as a result. Additionally, some of the manufacturers of name brands have begun to add premium foods to their product lines for those owners who are willing to spend more for higher quality. Premium foods are mostly found in pet supply and specialty stores.

Dog foods come in three textures: canned, semi-moist, and dry. Each has its benefits and drawbacks.

Canned Food

The advantages of canned food are that it is highly palatable and very conve-

> The type of dog food you'll need for your puppy will depend on his size and level of activity.

Make sure your puppy has cool clean water available at all times.

If you want to keep your puppies happy, remember to include some slight variation at mealtime. Several different flavors of canned food or a little something extra added to kibble will help to keep things interesting without upsetting the balance.

feeding your puppy

nient. It is also most appealing to owners, as canned food looks most like meat, which is what we think dogs like. Disadvantages are that it is expensive, that uneaten portions spoil if left out at room temperature, and it is most likely to lead to overeating if fed free-choice. Canned food also is the messiest food for dogs with beards and long ear fringes.

Semi-moist Food

Semi-moist food is lightweight, portable and very convenient. It requires no preparation or clean-up, will not spoil at room temperature, and is practically messless. Unfortunately, semi-

moist food contains many additives and preservatives, including sugars, in order to retain its moisture and not spoil. It is moderately expensive.

Dry Food

The least expensive food you can feed your puppy is dry food otherwise known as kibble. Dry food will not spoil at room temperature and therefore can be left out for the puppy to eat at his own pace. Dry food is easy to handle and helps promote healthy teeth and gums. On the negative side, dry food seems to be the least palatable of the three types of food unless fed from an early age.

An important reminder, even foods that will not spoil at room temperatures should not be left in your puppy's bowl indefinitely. A good rule of thumb is to discard uneaten portions at the end of every day.

Which texture food you feed is largely a personal choice—not so much your puppy's but yours—as he is likely to eat whatever you feed him. Mixing dry and canned foods together is a good way to obtain the benefits of both, and some packages include suggestions for how much of each to use. Semi-moist food, even if complete and balanced, should be avoided because of the additives it

---

The type of food you feed your puppy is generally up to you. After consulting your veterinarian and breeder choose a type of food that best suits your lifestyle and budget. Your puppy is likely to eat whatever you offer him.

contains. However, if you feed it just often enough so that it remains familiar to your dog's system, the handy, re-seal-able, single-portion packaging that requires no preparation or clean-up, probably makes it the most convenient food to use if you're traveling.

easier on digestion, would help maintain a consistent energy level, would avoid behavior problems associated with hunger and irritability, and would add interest to both ends of the day for your dog. Tiny breeds of dogs definitely should not be fed

to lick at the bowl after it's empty, you may be feeding too little. Keep in mind that these are rough estimates. Your puppy may need either a little more or a little less. Guide-lines are only that; your best guide to how much to feed your puppy is your puppy.

Puppies grow very quickly and the quantity of food you feed them should depend on their age as well as observation of your individual. If your puppy seems hungry even after he has consumed everything in his bowl, it is a safe assumption that he may need a larger serving.

How Much and How Often

Puppies under three months of age should be fed four times a day, puppies between three and six months three times, and puppies older than six months twice a day. After six months, your puppy should remain on two meals a day. Although for many years adult dogs were fed one meal a day, there seems to be little doubt that two meals a day would be

less than twice a day, no matter how old they are.

Use the feeding instruc-tions on the food package or can as a starting point in determining how much food to offer your puppy each day, but don't be so rigid about the guidelines that you forget to observe your own puppy. If he leaves food behind or picks at it slowly, chances are you're feeding him too much. If he gulps it down and continues

Remember it is important to talk to your breeder and veterinarian concerning dietary requirements and amounts as well.

At this age, a puppy prob-ably will not overeat, and if one or two meals are a little skimpy, the world won't end. Most importantly, check your dog's weight every few months so that you can correct any problems while they're still minor. To do a weight check,

feeding your puppy

run your hands lightly over your puppy's rib cage. You should be able to feel, not see, the bones beneath the skin.

A WORD ABOUT FREE-CHOICE FEEDING

Once your puppy has been housetrained, you may be tempted to leave dry food in his bowl at all times so that he can nibble at will. It is true that the practice of free-choice feeding eliminates a lot of frenzied behavior at meal-times because there are, in essence, no mealtimes. Nor will the puppy become irritable from hunger and inattentive due to low energy levels. Healthy puppies who happen to be poor eaters and have trouble maintaining their weight and energy, do well with free-choice feeding. On the other hand, free-choice feeding can lead to overeating and obesity and make it more difficult to monitor a dog's health and well-being by his appetite at mealtime.

SUPPLEMENTS

Supplements are intended to compensate for nutritional deficiencies, so you will not need to provide your puppy with any supplements unless instructed to do so by your veterinarian. A balanced diet provides all necessary nutrients in correct proportions.

SNACKS AND TREATS

Once your puppy is doing well on a regular feeding schedule, you can offer occasional snacks if there's some reason to do so. For instance, if you take an especially long walk one day, or if the puppy plays more vigorously than usual or has a particularly

exciting morning romping with a friend, these are occasions when a snack makes sense. Your puppy probably could use a little energy boost.

Treats, on the other hand, are best reserved as training aides. A food lure or treat is an effective way to induce a puppy to learn new behaviors or to reinforce behavior you want the puppy to retain. Offering treats at random times and for no apparent reason diminishes their effectiveness as training tools. Provide only wholesome, nutritious treats that are low in calories, such as pieces of raw vegetables, and bits of cheese or meat.

Keep in mind that both snacks and treats are still food. The caloric content of any snacks and treats offered

during the day must be taken into consideration and treats must be calculated as part of the daily ration.

TESTING THE DIET

The best test of any food is how well your puppy takes to it. When trying to establish a diet, ask these questions:
• Does he like it? The food your puppy loves best may not necessarily be the best for him. On the other hand, you should be able to find one that he likes that is good for him.
• Is the food easily and well digested by your puppy? Gas, bloating, loud gurgling noises after eating, loose, unformed stools, stools with undigested material in them, and very large stools are all signs that your puppy is not digesting the food particularly well. Look

Products that help eliminate bad breath for your pet are widely available at pet shops. The one shown here is chewable and works with the digestive system to help neutralize your pet's bad breath. Photo courtesy of Four Paws.

Be certain not to exercise your puppy immediately after he eats. Allow him time to digest his food properly.

feeding your puppy

Once your puppy is housetrained, you may be tempted to leave some dry food out at all times so he can nibble. Although this may sound harmless, it can lead to obesity as well as make it more difficult to judge your puppy's health by his appetite.

Feed your puppy in an out-of-the-way, but not isolated, place, and at roughly the same times every day. Get in the habit of feeding the puppy around the same time as the family eats, and to ask him or her to sit quietly while the food is prepared and placed on the floor.

Provide fresh water at all times. If the human members of your family are drinking bottled water, so should your puppy. Prevent a finicky eater by offering a variety of foods or at least a variety of flavors of the same brand. Alternate canned and dry portions or mix the two together.

Use mealtime as a way to monitor your puppy's health and overall well-being. Take note of any changes in appetite. Eating more or less for more than a few days could signal some kind of health problem that your veterinarian should check into.

for firm, well-formed, consistent stools.

• How does your puppy look overall? A shiny coat, clean skin (no flakes and scales), and clear eyes (no discharge) are good signs that your puppy's diet is agreeing with him.

FEEDING TIPS

First-time and even experienced puppy owners can make some basic mealtime mistakes.

Remember to avoid spicy, very rich, and fried foods, as well as sugary sweets. Foods in chunks large enough to choke, as well as poultry, fish or pork bones can prove vey dangerous. Also avoid foods that make your puppy hyperactive, very thirsty or seem to leave him hungry again in a short time. Avoid chocolate completely, it contains theo-

bromine, a substance that is poisonous to dogs. Also avoid giving your puppy milk, or onions, either raw or cooked.

Once your puppy is used to his regularly scheduled feedings, you can offer him occasional snacks. A tasty reward for good behavior or just a simple way to make him feel loved—a treat is always appreciated.

A well-socialized puppy enjoys the company and attention of people young and old. Socialization and training always go hand in paw!

PUPPY TRAINING

As you gaze into the warm eyes of your new puppy, it's easy to think of him as a baby with fur. Enjoy the feeling, but remind yourself of the truth. This puppy is a member of a different species and will need help fitting into a human family. There are three important ways that you can help him: socialization, handling and training.

SOCIALIZATION

The easiest way for your puppy to adapt to your lifestyle is through what we call socialization. Happily, the social skills your puppy will need, such things as being able to turn a deaf ear to the vacuum cleaner, a blind eye to the scampering kitten, and a tolerant attitude toward the letter carrier, are not built by drill, practice and hard work. All you have to do to help

Your new puppy is just like a baby; he will need you to teach him everything he needs to know to fit into his human family.

A well-socialized puppy will get along with everyone. He will enjoy meeting new people and keeping the company of other animals.

your puppy fit smoothly into your life is to gently and systematically introduce him to as many of the things that he will be expected to tolerate as a member of your family.

The first step is to think about the key characteristics of your lifestyle. Is it orderly and predictable? Chaotic and fast-paced? Do you travel a lot? Do you often bring strangers home? How often will your puppy come in contact with other dogs, cats or children? Will he be left home alone a lot? As you think about your lifestyle, jot down the kinds of sights, sounds and experiences your dog will encounter on a regular basis. Include such things as thunderstorms, fire sirens, loud music, the door bell, elevators, stairs, car trips, screaming children,

Handling a puppy is an important part of familiarizing him with the human world. If you are patient and gentle he will come to trust you and become used to handling.

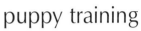

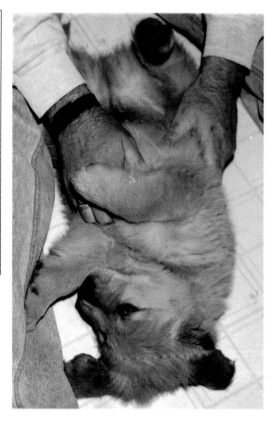

delivery people, cats, birds, horses, wildlife, the veterinarian and groomer.

The next step is to introduce him to those things in a way that will help him accept them calmly, rather than try to run away from them or attack them. In many cases, being exposed once or twice to something unfamiliar is all it takes. In others, it may take many repetitions and much patience on your part. The important thing is that you remain calm, low-key and encouraging. If he appears frightened at first, do not pick him up and baby him, and do not scold or reprimand him. Allow him to investigate and accept new things at his own pace.

HANDLING

If you want your adult dog to accept being groomed, examined by the veterinarian and treated when he is sick or injured—and all dogs really do need this skill—you need to accustom him to this kind of handling from an early age.

Handling is literally to touch, hold or manipulate with the hands. It includes affectionate handling, as in patting or stroking, and handling for a specific purpose, such as to examine, transport, treat, groom, or train. The only sure-fire way to make sure your puppy will grow up to accept specific kinds of handling is to introduce him to them when he is a puppy, in small stages over time, kindly but firmly and with encouragement and praise.

What kind of handling?

In order to hold his own in our world, the average dog will need to master the following kinds of hands-on experiences when the hands are his owner's, but also when they are the hands of a friendly stranger:

• Patting/stroking—for the pleasure of both dog and owner; as an aid in training.

• Handling of the eyes, ears, mouth—to examine, clean, or medicate.

• Handling of the whole body—to examine, massage, or treat; to lift, transport, restrain.

• Working with the coat—to examine and treat the skin or to groom.

• Bathing and drying—for general hygiene or in treatment of skin or other diseases.

• Handling of the feet and nails—to examine, treat, cleanse and trim.

It is necessary that your puppy be familiar with being touched and handled. Grooming and veterinary care require extensive manipulation of the puppy's body and the sooner he is used to this the better.

Accustoming your puppy to being handled in these ways will benefit both of you as well as other people who come in contact with him. In addition, teaching your puppy to be handled will make him that much easier to live with, train and enjoy.

TRAINING

In broad terms, teaching puppies what we need and/or want them to know is called training. Housetraining, socialization and handling all are forms of training, and are best begun on the very first day you bring your puppy home. The same is true of teaching your puppy obedience, or to have good manners. Puppies do best if they are trained both at home and in a class with other owners and puppies simultaneously.

It's almost never too soon to take yourself and your puppy to school! Puppy classes(also known as Puppy Play Groups), or KPT (Kindergarten Puppy Training) are for puppies over the age of eight weeks who have been fully immunized. Ideally, the whole family should participate. In puppy classes, which usually run for six or eight weeks, puppies not only begin to learn some basic commands such as to sit, come when called and walk on a leash, but they play and interact with many other puppies and are handled and socialized not only by their owners but by other adults, children, and the class trainers as well. Meanwhile, you can supplement class lessons by working on the basics at home.

Equipment
• A well-fitted buckle collar made of cotton or nylon, and a cotton or nylon leash either six or seven feet long.
• A small handful of your puppy's kibble, or bits of broken-up dog biscuits.

Picking a Time to Train
Pick a time when your puppy isn't exhausted from a play session, hasn't just eaten, and doesn't need to eliminate. Keep the sessions very short, a minute or two for very young puppies, and no more than five minutes for older ones.

Your Voice
Develop three distinct training voices to help your puppy distinguish your meaning. Commands should be given in a conversational tone, as if you were saying "I'm asking you to please sit."

Praise should be issued in a high-pitched and happy voice, as if you were saying "Hooray!"

Corrections should be spoken in a low-pitched, displeased tone. Pretend you're saying, "Just say No." Never shout at your puppy.

Enrolling your puppy in a kindergarten training class is a wonderful way to introduce your puppy to strangers. Not only will your pup learn basic commands and meet new people, he will have the invaluable camaraderie of his fellow puppies.

puppy training

Knowing When to Stop

No matter how long or short a training session has been, if your puppy begins to tire, get bored or antsy, it's time to stop. Try to end each session on a positive note, when your puppy has just succeeded at something and you've been able to praise him. Be mindful of your own mental state during training sessions; if you find yourself getting frustrated, impatient or inconsistent, it's definitely time to stop.

LAYING THE GROUNDWORK FOR TRAINING

First, make sure to teach your puppy her name. Say it in an upbeat voice, and praise her warmly and/or give her a treat for looking toward you. Then, familiarize your puppy with wearing a collar. She may take to it immediately, or you may have to introduce it in steps and stages until she is wearing it full-time.

Over the course of a few days, get the puppy used to being on leash. At first, let her drag it around until she becomes nonchalant about the weight hanging from her collar. Be sure to discourage chewing the leash, if necessary apply a product that will make the leash taste unpleasant. After that, hold the end of the leash and let her discover the different sensations of pulling against it and

having it hang loosely when she stays close to your side. Entice her with your voice to stay close, and praise her whenever she moves in such as way that a taut leash becomes looser.

Correct your puppy by giving a quick tug/release on the leash and saying no. The only purpose of the tug is to get the puppy's attention. The real correction is in the disapproving tone of your voice.

TEACHING THE SIT

Attach your puppy's leash to her collar. With your puppy standing, position yourself along one of her sides—if you are right-handed, it probably will be easier if she is on your left—hold a bit of food high over her head and move your hand slightly to the rear. Say

"Sit." As she raises her head to follow your hand, her body may automatically lower into a sit. If so, praise her immediately and give her a tidbit.

Repeat the command and action the same way several more times. She will quickly associate the word sit with the action on her part that gets her the praise and the treat.

If your puppy doesn't sit, she gets no tidbit and no praise. Simply look and move slightly away from her and wait several minutes before trying again. Do not even think about correcting her for not sitting at this point. Corrections are only appropriate when your puppy knows what to do but doesn't do it.

If your puppy doesn't automatically sit when the morsel is above her head, try gently pulling up on the leash

There is no better reward after a hard day's training than a Nylabone®.

with your right hand and sliding your left hand across her hind legs, tuck her legs under at the knees as you say sit. Even the beginning of a squat is cause for praise. Try again and be ready with your enthusiastic praise for all moves in the right direction. Correctly timed praise should come as your puppy is deciding to sit. That way she'll more quickly connect what she's doing with the reward she gets from you. Use your hands on your puppy as little as possible. They really learn a lot better and faster if they move their bodies into position by themselves.

TEACHING THE STAY

Only begin teaching the stay when your puppy reliably performs the sit. Proceed in stages; do not move forward to the next stage until your puppy knows the one you're working on now.

Stand on your puppy's right side, with the leash attached to her collar. Ask her to sit. Praise her for sitting. Immediately slide the palm of your left hand down and backward to a point just in front of your puppy's nose. Say "Stay," as you do so. If your puppy stays for a second or two, praise her calmly and slowly, excited praise may cause her to jump up, then release her and let her wander off.

If your puppy doesn't stay, give a gentle tug on the leash while saying "No." This should just startle her a little. As she hesitates, ask her to sit again, praise her, and again give the hand signal and verbal command, "sStay." If she stays at all, praise her immediately.

As the puppy begins to understand that stay means to remain sitting, and eventually stays every time for five or ten seconds, you can begin with your right foot to walk a little bit away from her. The right foot, being further away from your puppy, is less likely to tempt her to move out when you do. Should she begin to get up, give a tug on the leash, say "No," replace her in the sit, praise, and try the stay again.

Gradually increase the distance that you walk away after giving the stay command until your puppy will remain in place while you go the length of the leash. Don't repeat the stay command more than two or three times

> The first command your puppy will work on is the sit. One of the easiest to learn, all the other commands build on her knowledge of this one. As you suspend a treat directly over her head say, "Sit." Upon looking up at the treat, her rear end will go down. After several repetitions of this your pup will get the idea.

Praise is very important during training. Your puppy must know you are pleased if he is to keep trying. Praise your puppy warmly and often.

After your puppy performs the sit command well, you can move on to the stay. Stay requires that your puppy remain in a seated position while you leave his side.

in one training session. Very gradually increase the time the puppy is asked to stay, to about one minute by the time she is six months old.

TEACHING THE DOWN

Begin with your puppy in a sitting position with the leash attached to her collar. Using a bit of food as a lure, hold the food between your puppy's front legs, directly under her nose, and slowly lower your hand to the ground and then drag it along the ground away from her as you say, "Down." Don't get too far in front of your puppy's nose, or she will get up. Praise the puppy for any attempt she makes at obeying the down command. If instead of going down, the puppy gets up from the sit, give a tug on the leash, say "No," ask her to sit again, praise, then once again attempt the down sequence.

Once your puppy goes down, squat next to her, looking away, and try to get her to relax in that position. Release her by saying "Okay!" Praise her enthusiastically.

TEACHING THE COME

Begin teaching the come command with your puppy on leash. Practice in locations where there are few or no distractions. From just a few feet away from your puppy, crouch down on her level, open your arms, call her name and then say "Come" in a very excited voice. Praise the puppy as soon as she begins to move toward you, continuing until she has reached you.

For puppies who do not come readily to this encouragement, try getting their attention and then either running away while calling them to come, or backing away facing them. Praise them as soon as they move toward you and continue as long as they are on their way. Look away and stop praising if the puppy stops and wanders off. You do not want to repeat the command if you hope to have your puppy come on the first time the command is given, which can be important for safety's sake. Once your puppy knows the come command, you can begin to correct her gently for failing to come when called, gently give the leash a tug. When you've gotten her attention, repeat the come command with open arms and happy praise for any forward motion.

TEACHING TO WALK ON LEASH

To get your puppy to walk along happily at your side, you have to be interesting. Say her name, pat your leg and then say "Let's go!" to get her started. Make sure the leash stays slack, and do

The down command is more difficult for puppies to learn. Fortunately, with the help of a food treat and patience, your puppy will relax in no time.

Extensive training may lead your puppy to life as a working dog. This German Shepherd puppy is on his way to becoming an aide to the handicapped.

everything you can to get and keep her attention. Praise her for keeping up with you, talk to her, give her the occasional bit of food, keep up a brisk pace, change directions frequently, make lots of zigs and zags, and keep the lessons short (only a minute or two).

Once your puppy knows what "Let's go!" means, you can begin to use a short tug on the leash to correct her for not moving out when you do. Whenever she stops walking to sniff the ground, or veers off in another direction, say "No," give the leash a tug, repeat the words "Let's go!" and praise her when she once again begins to walk with you.

There are many additional commands that you can teach your puppy to make life together more pleasant. Some examples are "Off," when you want her to get off the furniture; "Leave it," when you want her to drop something she's picked up or gone over to, to investigate; and "Up," to encourage her up into the car

Remember, your puppy comes to you as a blank slate, waiting for you to teach him. The time you spend training will dictate the quality of life you have together in the future.

or onto another surface. Training doesn't have to be limited to useful commands. The same techniques of lure and reward can be used to

teach your puppy to shake hands, give kisses, play "Find it" games and as many other fun activities as you can think of.

A healthy treat for your puppy because they love cheese. This product, called Chooz™, is bone hard but it can be micro-waved to make it expand into a huge, crisp dog biscuit. It is almost fat free with about 70% protein.

The POPpup™ is a healthy treat for your puppy. Its bone-hard structure helps control plaque mechanically. If microwaved, it becomes a rich cracker that your puppy will love. POPpup™ are available in liver and other flavors. They are fortified with calcium, too.

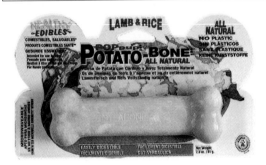

Grooming allows for quiet time between you and your puppy, helps you get some insight into the health of your pup, and allows you to identify and eradicate any external parasites. Best of all, your pup will look and smell his best.

her to do this while she's young! Puppies who miss this part of their early training may resist the brush, comb and nail clippers for the rest of their lives. By comparison, when introduced at a young age, grooming can become a soothing ritual for you both.

Depending on your puppy's coat type and where you acquired her, she may or may not have been introduced already to the basics of being groomed: a little light brushing, having her nails clipped, a bit of scissoring around ears and feet, maybe even her first bath. If so, you're ahead of the game. If not, the time to start is now. It doesn't matter if your puppy's coat is nothing but peach fuzz; it's her attitude about the process that you're "grooming" at this point.

No matter what type of coat your puppy has, he or she must be groomed on a regular basis. Puppies with smooth coats, such as Dachshunds, Beagles, Rottweilers, and Pit Bulls, for example, and many mixed breeds, will require minimal brushing and combing, whereas Poodles, Yorkshire Terriers, Cocker Spaniels and Schnauzers will need extensive grooming to keep their coats clean and untangled. Nevertheless, right now the primary purpose of daily grooming your puppy is to accustom her to being handled all over. As you familiarize yourself with your puppy's body, she must learn to stand or lie still, to have her teeth brushed and her nails cut. You will be thankful forever for teaching

A wide range of shampoos exists to meet any dog's needs, from flea and tick to specially medicated to whitening and brightening and more. All shampoos are pH balanced for a gentle yet effective cleaning. Photo courtesy of Four Paws.

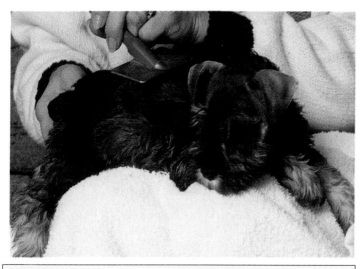

Depending upon the breed of puppy you choose, you will need special grooming tools.

body from side to side as necessary. Others groom with their puppy standing on a stool, table, or countertop. If you already know that there will be a lot of grooming in your puppy's life, you may want to bite the bullet now and purchase a professional grooming table, available at pet supply stores and through mail-order catalogs. You will find that there's less strain on your back if you can sit or stand and have your puppy on a surface at waist height. If you do groom your puppy on a table, particularly a professional grooming table with a post and neck noose, be aware that you cannot take your eyes or hands off the puppy for one single second. Puppies and adult dogs alike have been injured and even killed by jumping off countertops and grooming tables. If a puppy jumps while her head is inside a noose, she can hang herself.

WHAT YOU'LL NEED

No matter what breed or type of dog your puppy is, you don't need a lot of fancy supplies to get started. If you find yourself really "getting into" the grooming thing, you may want to invest in additional supplies. For now, the following should suffice:

• A medium-soft bristle brush, for puppies with long hair, or rubber curry brush, for puppies with smooth coats.

• A stainless steel comb for puppies with long hair.

• A fine-tooth or flea comb.

• Scissors with blunt tips.

• Shampoo made for puppies.

• A sponge.

• Nail clippers made for dogs.

• A toothbrush and flavored toothpaste made for dogs.

• Cotton balls; towels.

• A non-slip mat.

• A spray attachment for faucet.

• A hair dryer (optional.)

SETTING UP

Before you begin, give a little thought to where you will do the grooming. Some people train tiny puppies to lay in their laps or on a table for grooming, turning the

Your dog will need a special brush depending on his coat length or skin condition. There are slicker brushes, pin brushes, curry brushes—something to suit the needs of any dog. Photo courtesy of Four Paws.

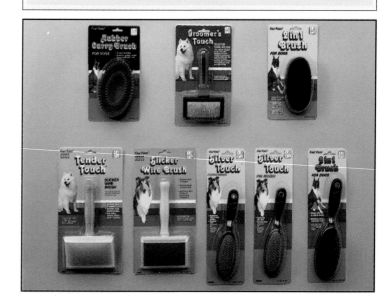

No matter what type of coat your puppy has, grooming is necessary for the health of his skin and coat.

When you first begin grooming your puppy, you can find everything you'll need at your local pet shop. The basics will do just fine to get you started.

or impatient. If you concentrate on explaining to your puppy what you're doing and why, even though she won't understand a single word, you will have automatically adopted the right no-nonsense tone.

Don't give your puppy a rawhide chew or other toy to distract her while you groom. She really does have to learn that this is a serious matter. Praise her calmly for every few seconds that she is calm and cooperative. And don't ever let her convince you to put down the comb, brush or clippers when she says so; that only teaches her that if she squirms and struggles, you'll stop.

Once you've picked the spot where you will do your grooming, gather together all your supplies so you can proceed in an orderly fashion. Incidentally, don't attempt a full-scale session for several weeks. It will pay off in the long run if you start off slowly and spend just a few seconds on each maneuver.

ESTABLISHING A ROUTINE

Just as with feeding, walking and training, you will want to establish a routine for grooming that your puppy can learn to depend on. It doesn't matter so much what you do first and what you do second, but try to groom your puppy in pretty much the same way at each session. For example, you might begin by running the brush gently over the puppy's legs, body and head, all in about 10 seconds, then go back over the same areas, in the same order, with the comb, taking another 10 seconds. As you work, talk softly and calmly to the

puppy. You don't want to wheedle or plead with her to stand still (this probably is out of the question anyway!), nor do you want to get gruff

GROOMING ESSENTIALS

Some of the following procedures (combing, trimming) will apply only to

It's as important for our animal friends to have healthy teeth and gums as it is for us. Fortunately, maintaining oral care is getting easier and easier for the pet owner. Now there's a taste-free, easy-to-use gel that will keep pets' teeth clean, reduce tartar build up, and eliminate breath odor. Photo courtesy of Breath Friend™/American Media Group.

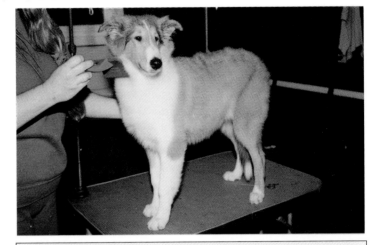

puppies with long hair, but others (brushing, bathing, clipping nails and cleaning teeth) apply to all puppies.

Brushing and Combing

Always brush your puppy first. This separates the hair, distributes oils, and feels good. If your puppy has hair of any length, follow up with the comb. Work slowly and carefully from the tips of the hair back toward the puppy's body, feeling for tangles or small matted areas as you go. If you encounter resistance, stop. Grasp the problem area with your fingers, lifting the coat to make sure you release any tension against the dog's skin. Then break up any snarls or mats with your fingers, the brush, or the tip of the comb. Only when you can comb cleanly through the area that was snarled or matted should you release your grip on the coat and comb from the skin outward. Correct and thorough combing is the key to managing long, flowing coats, thick bushy coats, and wiry/curly coats.

When you're through, the comb should run through smoothly, from the skin to the tips of the hair. Not just down the center of your puppy's back, but everywhere: in the armpits, on the insides of the rear legs, behind the ears, on the tops of the feet, and at the corners of the mouth. If yours is a puppy whose coat is just beginning to grow, you shouldn't encounter anything too serious, although eating and drinking can mat the hair around the mouth, as stepping in urine puddles can mat the hair on the rear feet. During your first grooming

Establish a grooming routine with your puppy that she can depend on. Try to groom her in the same way each time. Do not allow your puppy to become impatient, and do not distract her with a toy. If she struggles praise her calmly and continue to groom. Only when you are finished should the grooming session be over.

sessions, only tackle one small tangle at a time, then move on.

If you find that secretions from the eyes or food particles around the mouth are becoming stuck in your puppy's facial hair, moisten a cotton ball with warm water and squeeze it into the soiled areas. Let the water soften the material for a few minutes while you work elsewhere on the body, then go back and comb the debris out of the hair with a fine-tooth or flea comb.

Dental products are available for helping to fight plaque, reduce tartar build-up and control unpleasant breath in dogs. Photo courtesy of Four Paws.

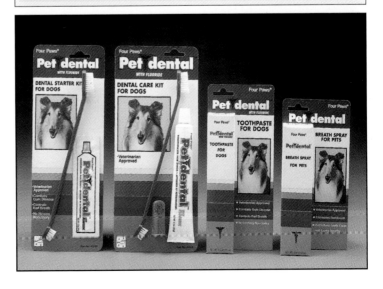

Trimming

Puppies with hair around their eyes, ears and mouth, around their anal/genital area, and on their feet, need to be trimmed. Depending on the age of your puppy, right now you may be snipping air, but it's important for your puppy to get used to the feel and sound of the scissors.

Feet: Stand your puppy on a table and scissor all the way around each foot. When she lifts the foot you're working on (and she will, because dogs are sensitive around their feet), lift the opposite one instead and hold it up. Lift each foot, place the scissors flat against the pad, and snip any hair that extends beyond the pad (be careful not to pinch the pad with the scissors.) Put the scissors down when she's standing quietly, not when she's resisting.

Eyes: Grasp the puppy's muzzle to keep her head steady, and scissor short any long hair hanging over the eyes. Be careful not to cut away hair that grows on the muzzle between the eyes, as the cut hairs can irritate the eye as they grow back in.

Ears: Trim away the hair that grows beyond the edges of the ears. Don't worry about getting right up to the edge until you're more comfortable with the scissors. Your puppy probably will be wiggling and tossing her head; don't try to forcibly restrain her. Concentrate on holding the ear gently but firmly, talking calmly, and going through the motions until she figures out this isn't going to hurt.

Mouth: Puppies with a lot of hair on their muzzles and chins are destined to having their faces washed several times a day or to having the hair trimmed short for reasons of good hygiene.

Anal/genital region: Your puppy will stay cleaner longer if you get in the habit of cutting away the hair that grows around the rectum and genital areas. Practice the motions before you actually cut any hair. Scissoring the genital area is easiest with the dog lying on his or her back, either in your lap or on a table.

Bathing

Bathe your puppy in a warm room, away from drafts. Puppy's first baths will be stressful, so pick a day when nothing else is going on and when the puppy is feeling well and eating well. After her bath, your puppy will need to relieve herself, then have a nice long rest.

Unless your puppy is very large, plan to bathe her in the kitchen sink so you don't have to bend over, which creates considerable strain on the back. Place the non-slip mat in the sink, then cut a hole over the drain so the water can run out. Attach the hose to the faucet and experiment until the temperature is warm and the water flow is light to moderate. Put small plugs of cotton in each of your puppy's ears, then stand her on the mat in the sink and reassure her for a minute.

Thoroughly wet the coat and the underside of the puppy. Use the sponge to wet her head and face. Shampoo the body, add a bit more water, and use your fingers to work up a lather (don't rub long hair in circles as this causes matting.) Wash down each leg and under the feet. Wash the head last by applying the shampoo to the sponge. Try to avoid getting shampoo in the eyes or mouth. Then rinse the whole dog thoroughly, first the body

> Owners of dogs with ear problems can choose from a variety of ear care products, from cleaners to remedies for proper ear hygiene. Photo courtesy of Four Paws.

grooming your puppy

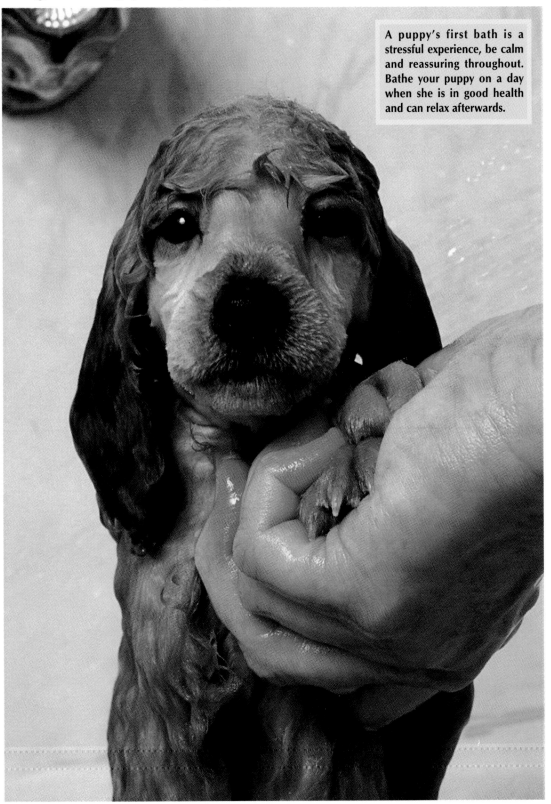

A puppy's first bath is a stressful experience, be calm and reassuring throughout. Bathe your puppy on a day when she is in good health and can relax afterwards.

it will bleed if you nick it, and it will hurt, and your puppy will never forget it. As with other grooming procedures, praise the puppy for cooperative behavior and don't let her think that you'll stop if she resists.

Cleaning Teeth

Using flavored toothpaste for dogs and either a toothbrush, a finger-brush (available in pet supply stores) or even a piece of gauze or rough cloth wrapped around your forefinger, gently pull your puppy's upper lip away from the teeth with one hand and brush a few teeth and the gum area with the toothbrush. Then pull away the lower lip and do the same. Spend just a few seconds at first, but gradually increase

Never bathe your puppy in a cold or drafty room. Only on a warm summer's day should a bath take place outside.

and legs, then underneath, then the head. Make sure every trace of shampoo is out of the hair.

Place your puppy on one towel and dry her gently with the other, squeezing as much water as possible into the towel. Either let the puppy air-dry, or dry her with the hairdryer (not too hot and not too close to the skin), brushing her coat as it dries.

Clipping Nails

Nails can be clipped when they're dry, but dogs seem to mind it less when they're soft from the bath. Begin by just doing one or two at a time, and take off only the tiny bit that curves down at the tip (viewed from the underside). On puppies with black nails, you won't be able to see the vein or "quick" inside; this vein does not extend past the curved portion of the nail, but

Be sure to thoroughly dry your puppy after his bath. Use a towel to remove excess water and then allow him to air dry or use a hairdryer made especially for dogs.

grooming your puppy

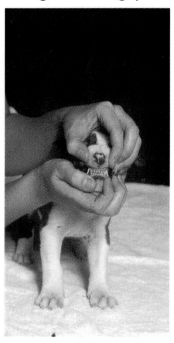

easier than trying to correct a coat neglected for months. Consider this schedule:

• Brushing and combing—every day.

• Cleaning the beard and under the eyes—every day.

• Brushing the teeth—every day.

• Clipping nails—once a week.

• Bathing—once a month or as needed.

• Trimming the coat—every two months.

WHAT ABOUT PROFESSIONAL GROOMING?

There is no denying that it is very time-consuming to care for some coats, especially if you want to leave the hair long rather than keep it cut short, and eventually you may decide to have your puppy's coat clipped, trimmed and bathed by a professional. Even if you do, brushing and combing as well as teeth and nail care still should be performed regularly at home.

the time you spend brushing the teeth until you are able to do the whole mouth at one time. To prevent tartar build-up and eventual "dog breath," the teeth should be brushed every day.

Finishing Touches

If your puppy has enough hair above her eyes for a topknot, comb it up and fasten it in a rubber band or clasp. Make sure the hair isn't pulled tight and that you don't accidentally catch any skin in the rubber band. Small ribbons or bits of yarn can be added if you like.

How Often?

Spending a few minutes a day to keep your puppy well-groomed, especially if she has long hair, is much

Undoubtedly, the minute your puppy is out of your sight after you've groomed him, he'll find a mess to get into—that's a puppy, take it all in stride!

KEEPING YOUR PUPPY HEALTHY

As important as it is to select a basically healthy puppy and to find a good veterinarian, the most critical factor in the on-going health of your puppy is you. Making sure he or she gets regular preventive care from a veterinarian is part of it, but providing a healthy diet, daily exercise, regular grooming, and appropriate lifestyle are just as important. Beyond that, it's up to you to know what's normal for your puppy so you'll know what isn't and when to seek professional help, as well as what to do in an emergency.

FIRST VISIT

You should take your new puppy to the veterinarian almost immediately after his arrival. Take along a stool specimen to be tested for worm eggs. Write down ahead of time any questions that you have, and bring along a notebook to write down the answers as well as any instructions that the veterinarian gives you.

Review with your veterinarian the types of vaccines your puppy has had, as this will determine when the next series is due. Although there is currently a debate going on

about if, when, and how often to immunize puppies, most experts agree that puppies should be vaccinated at least once against the major contagious diseases that affect dogs, such as distemper, hepatitis and parvovirus. Vaccination against rabies is required by law in all 50 states.

Other subjects to discuss with your veterinarian at your first visit are any local veterinary issues you should be aware of, such as whether you need to be concerned about heartworms or Lyme disease. Ask the veterinarian to dem-

A healthy puppy is a happy puppy. In order to ensure the health of your young canine companion, schedule him for regular veterinary visits.

onstrate anything you're unsure about, such as how much nail to clip off when you're grooming, how to open the puppy's mouth, clean his ears and take his temperature. If the veterinarian does not provide emergency care, find out which emergency clinic he uses.

After your puppy is fully immunized, you may not see the veterinarian again for a year. In all likelihood, you will receive reminders when he is due for follow-up visits. Normally this is on an annual basis, but depending on where you live and travel, and what your puppy is exposed to, a different schedule may be recommended.

REGULAR VETERINARY CARE

In addition to annual checkups and booster shots, get in the habit of taking your puppy to the veterinarian anytime something seems wrong to you. Outright signs of illness, such as vomiting or diarrhea more than once or twice, fever, limping or obvious pain anywhere, shaking the head or pawing at the eyes, foul breath that may or may not be accompanied by drooling, hesitancy to eat hard foods and reluctance to be handled around the mouth, rapid or labored breathing, discharge or bleeding from any body opening, seizures or prolonged trembling all are sure signs that your dog needs to see his doctor.

Make a point of finding out what your puppy's normal temperature, pulse rate and respiration rate are, and write them down somewhere so you will always know when any of his vital statistics are high or low. Likewise, any change in behavior is cause for attention; changes that persist for longer than about 24 hours should send you to the veterinarian. Incidentally, the more

---

Your puppy's veterinarian should provide a thorough examination each time you visit. Aside from inoculations and vital statistics, your vet should examine your puppy for external parasites and any complaint you may have apprised him of. Your veterinarian should always be willing to answer any questions and demonstrate procedures you do not understand.

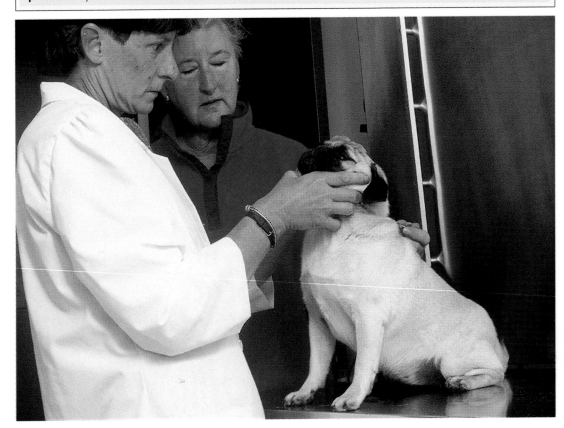

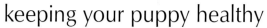

keeping your puppy healthy

thoroughly you know your dog's usual attitude, activity level, appetite, stool and urine output, sleep habits and other behaviors, the more likely you will be to quickly notice any changes. Just as with people, early diagnosis of a problem usually leads to a more satisfactory (and less expensive) outcome.

PEST CONTROL

Parasites are living things—generally insects, bugs, worms, and microscopic organisms called protozoa—that must live in or on a host animal, your puppy, in order to survive. Some parasites do no harm, some are nuisances, and some cause serious disease, even death. A few can also infect humans. We divide parasites into internal and external types, depending on whether they live in or on your dog's body. It is difficult or impossible to prevent your puppy from ever playing host to any parasites, particularly if he spends much time out of doors, and it is equally difficult to eliminate every single worm or bug that lands on your puppy. A more realistic goal is to be ever-vigilant about parasites and to initiate treatment before a full-blown infestation occurs. In some cases there are effective parasite prevention medications that you can give your puppy on a regular basis or seasonally. Below there is a list and description of the most common parasites that may infect your puppy.

Internal Parasites

Roundworms: Adult roundworms are slender white parasites that live in the intestines of dogs (and many other mammals) and measure from one to several inches in length. They feed on ingested food in the intestines, robbing the host of nutrition. Symptoms of roundworm infestation in dogs include a pot-bellied yet emaciated appearance, dull, dry coat, ravenous appetite and foul diarrhea. Adult roundworms are passed from the body in the puppy's vomit or feces, where they are often discovered by the owner. Worm eggs are shed in the feces of infected dogs, where they can be picked up by other dogs and by children who play in contaminated soil. Almost all adult dogs harbor some roundworms, which nursing females pass on to their puppies. Even if your puppy has no symptoms of roundworms, expect that he or she probably has some and on your first visit to the veterinarian, bring

> Regular visits to your vet will not only prove beneficial to your puppy's health—he may even come to enjoy them!

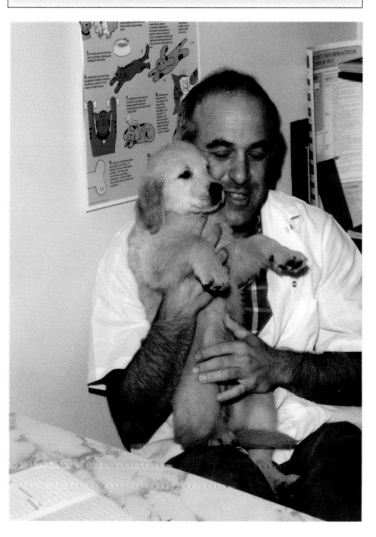

Once a day, perhaps while grooming, be sure to examine your puppy for fleas and ticks as well as symptoms of other parasites.

in a stool sample.

Hookworms: Hookworms are also intestinal parasites, so named because of the hook-like teeth they use to attach themselves to the intestinal wall. They not only rob the puppy or dog of nutrition, but also suck blood. Puppies with heavy infestations can actually die of anemia due to blood loss. Hookworms are passed from dog to dog through feces in

much the same way as roundworms are, although hookworm larvae can also burrow through the skin of young puppies. Unlike roundworms, hookworms are too small to be readily noticed by the naked eye. Symptoms of hookworm infestation are the same as for roundworms, with the additional symptom of the pale mucous membranes that signal the presence of anemia.

Whipworms: A third intestinal parasite, the whipworm lives and feeds in the colon of puppies and dogs. Puppies are infected by eating egg-infested feces or licking their paws after walking through feces-contaminated soil. Symptoms include colitis (inflammation of the colon), abdominal bloating and gas, bloody and/or mucous-coated stools, diarrhea, insatiable appetite and emaciated appearance.

Tapeworms: Tapeworms are flat and white and shed egg-filled independent segments of themselves in bowel movements. The telltale twisting segments may be seen clinging to the puppy or dog's hair around the anus or in a fresh stool sample. The primary symptoms of tapeworms in dogs are weight loss despite a voracious appetite as well as rectal itching and the presence of live segments around the rectum. Dogs contract tapeworms by eating infected fleas, which are intermediary hosts, and by eating the raw meat of infected mice and other rodents.

Heartworms: As their name suggests, these spaghetti-like worms measuring several to many inches in length live not in the intestines but in the chambers of

Hookworms are passed from puppies through contact with an infected pup's feces. They attach themselves to the walls of the intestines and rob the puppy of nutrition and blood.

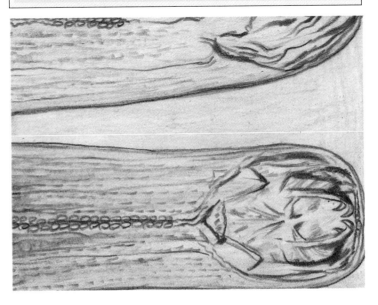

keeping your puppy healthy

Whipworms are hard to find, and it is a job best left to a veterinarian. Pictured here are adult whipworms.

the heart and the blood vessels of the lungs. Symptoms include a persistent cough, especially upon exertion, weight loss and general body weakness. As increasing numbers of worms—from a few dozen up to 100—mature inside the heart and lungs, the dog eventually will develop congestive heart failure and obstructive pulmonary disease. Dogs contract heartworm disease only one way, through the bite of larvae-infected mosquitoes, but it can take from six months to several years after infection for symptoms to develop. Fortunately, there is now a heartworm preventative on the market which, because of the seriousness of the disease, is administered year-round in areas of the country where mosquitoes are found. A significant benefit of heartworm medication is that it appears to also control other kinds of worms. A puppy's first visit to the veterinarian is not too soon to ask about

heartworm prevention.

Giardia canis and Coccidia: These are two different protozoan parasites that infect the intestines and cause abdominal bloating, loose, watery or bloody diarrhea, mucous-coated stools, and weight loss. Both are spread through infected feces of dogs or other animals. Giardia is also found in outdoor water supplies in some areas of the country and can be contracted when dogs drink the water.

External Parasites

Fleas: Unfortunately, the flea is familiar to us all. Easily visible to the naked eye, the flea is a very fast-moving brown insect about the size of a sesame seed. Fleas are caught from other dogs or from cats that have them and usually are found at the base of the dog's tail, between the legs, and on the abdomen and thighs, where they suck the blood of their hosts, leaving behind black specks of dirt

that is actually their feces. Flea saliva is very irritating to dogs and flea bites can cause intense itching, redness and swelling. Highly allergic dogs will scratch relentlessly for weeks from a single bite, often causing hair loss and secondary bacterial infections. Fleas will also bite humans, usually on the ankles and lower legs, causing the same red swellings and intense itching. As noted above, fleas may carry the larvae of tapeworms, infecting your dog with that parasite. Effective control of a heavy infestation of fleas usually involves treating the dog, the home and the yard simultaneously, as some stages of the flea's life cycle are spent off the dog. New and highly effective insecticides against fleas are always coming on the market. Discuss the best method for controlling fleas with your

Dirofilaria- adult worms in the heart of a dog. It is possible for a dog to be infected with any number of worms from one to a hundred. Courtesy of Merck AgVet.

The flea is a brown insect the size of a sesame seed that sucks the blood of its host. Flea saliva is tremendously irritating to puppies and can cause severe itching and sometimes skin irritation.

ear canal where they feed on the outer layers of the skin and leave behind a crumbly dark brown residue that resembles coffee grounds and often is the visible sign of their presence. Dogs with ear mites furiously scratch or paw at their ears and shake their heads. Speak to your veterinarian if you suspect ear mites. Treatment consists of flushing out the ear canal and then applying an insecticide to kill the mites. Other mites live in or on the skin or inside

veterinarian.

Ticks: Dogs are plagued by several different kinds of ticks, which are round black bugs of various sizes that attach themselves to the dog's body and feed on its blood over a course of hours or even days. Ticks are found outdoors, primarily in wooded and grassy areas, and they drop down onto your dog (or you) as you walk by. Tick bites rarely cause the kind of itching that flea bites do, but ticks do transmit several serious diseases, including Rocky Mountain Spotted Fever and Lyme Disease. Products that are effective for flea control usually are only partially effective against ticks. Ask your veterinarian what product he recommends for control of ticks.

Mites: There are several different kinds of mites that you should be aware of. All dogs seem to have small numbers of mites (passed on by their mothers) but in some individuals, perhaps when the immune system is weak, the population begins to increase dramatically, causing skin disease. Ear mites, as their name suggests, live inside the

Demodex mites, commonly known as ear mites, live inside the ear and feed on the outer layers of skin where they leave a dark brown, crumbling residue. Puppies with ear mites will become intolerably uncomfortable if left untreated.

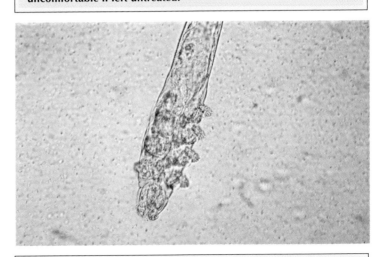

Sarcoptic mites live on the skin of puppies and cause intense itching and an array of skin diseases, some of which are very severe.

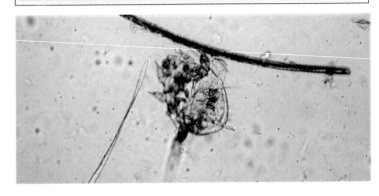

keeping your puppy healthy

Puppies can contract a host of parasites just from being exposed to the outdoors. Be sure to check your puppy thoroughly before he comes into the house.

hair follicles on the dog's body (anywhere except in the ears!) and cause intense itching and skin diseases called manges, which can vary in severity and some of which are highly contagious to other dogs and people. Very advanced cases of certain manges can cause death. Treatment can be prolonged and messy. Do not ignore a puppy's persistent scratching, it may be nothing but always bears investigating by your veterinarian.

Lice: Lice cling to the hair shafts and feed on the skin and/or the blood of their hosts. Lice lay eggs, called nits, which are firmly attached to the hair shafts and look like small white dots. Lice cause intense itching, hair loss, and sometimes anemia as well from loss of blood. As these symptoms may mimic those of other external parasites, you need to have your veterinarian determine if they are caused by lice. Lice are spread from dog to dog in situations where crowding occurs (shelters, kennels). Treatment is relatively easy using an insecticide for fleas or ticks.

SAFETY MEASURES

You can do much to assure the health of your puppy by proofing any area in which the dog will spend time. Puppies explore the environment with their mouths, often swallowing things without even intending to. And while they are teething, they will attempt to chew virtually anything that they can get their jaws around. This means that you must scrutinize any rooms or outdoor areas that the puppy has access to with a sharp eye out

A puppy will forever find his own adventure and mischief. To avoid problems, provide your puppy with safe and appropriate toys.

There are many kinds of flying disks for puppies and children, but only one brand is made just for dogs with strength, scent, and originality. The Nylabone® Frisbee™ is a must if you want to have this sort of fun with your puppy. *The trademark Frisbee is used under liscence from Mattell, Inc. California, U.S.A.

keeping your puppy healthy

It is important to ensure the safety of your puppy when traveling in the car. Restrain him with a specially made harness seatbelt or confine him to a travel crate.

for hazards. As the puppy reaches one year of age, the relentless chewing will begin to abate and you can relax your guard a little.

Common hazards in the home and yard include kitchen cleansers, insecticides and fertilizers, weed killers and snail bait, anti-freeze, prescription and over-the-counter drugs, wood and paint chips and the pressurized wood used in decks and children's play structures. Puppies will ingest items as incomprehensible as bolts and washers, fishing line, twist ties on garbage bags (not to mention the garbage itself),

It's a fact—puppies, just like babies, will put everything into their mouths for exploration! In order to keep your puppy safe, do not allow him access to any object small enough to be ingested.

pantyhose, coins, marbles, and women's sanitary products. Many household and ornamental plants and outdoor shrubs are toxic to dogs; if in doubt, make sure your puppy cannot get at them. Likewise, keep your puppy away from electrical and telephone cords, and from synthetic fabrics that may contain toxic materials.

Car safety includes restraining your puppy with a specially designed safety harness attached to your automobile's seat belt, or inside a sturdy dog crate. Never leave your puppy unattended in a car during the warm weather. Both in the car and at home, offer the puppy safe and appropriate chew toys made for dogs. Don't automatically assume, however, that all dog toys are automatically safe for your puppy. Many contain small parts that can be chewed off and swallowed, and toys and balls made of latex or vinyl may be no match for your own puppy's chewing power. If yours is a power chewer, stick with hard rubber or nylon, or with natural, unbleached domestic rawhide.

EMERGENCIES AND FIRST AID

No matter how careful you are, accidents still can happen. Be prepared with an all-purpose first-aid kit for your dog. These are now available commercially and through catalogs; ask at your local pet-supply store. Ask your veterinarian to show you how to perform basic first-aid procedures such as putting on a tourniquet in case of bleeding, splinting a broken leg, transporting your puppy if he's injured, or, in a worst-case scenario, performing CPR. Alternatively, there are videos on the market that demonstrate various first-aid techniques. Also, be sure you know the location and telephone number of the off-hours emergency service that your veterinarian recommends. Drive there sometime as a rehearsal, just to make sure you can find your way quickly if you need to. Most emergencies affecting your dog can be prevented by common sense and good judgment (yours, not his!), such as set forth in the puppy-proofing section, above.

Finally, recognize an emergency when you have one, and take prompt action. Uncontrollable bleeding, continuous vomiting or diarrhea, extremely labored breathing, convulsions, sudden paralysis, shock — these are emergencies and your dog's life may depend on your response. Call your veterinarian immediately, describe the situation and rush your dog to the clinic.

HOW TO GIVE MEDICATIONS TO YOUR PUPPY

To give a pill: open the mouth by placing your thumb behind the canine tooth. Press upward against the roof of the mouth. With the other hand, place the pill in the center of the mouth, as far back as possible. Give a little push over the back of the tongue. Close the mouth and hold it closed until the puppy swallows.

To give liquids: Use an eyedropper or syringe. Usually this will come with the medication. Make sure the puppy's mouth is closed. Tilt the chin up to about 45 degrees, and

insert the eyedropper into the natural pocket. between the puppy's teeth and cheek. If there's any excess flesh, hold it closed around the eyedropper with your fingers. Squeeze the bulb of the eyedropper, and hold the puppy's muzzle firmly closed until she swallows.

WHAT TO DO IN CASE OF CHOKING

If there are two people present, have one drive to the emergency clinic while the other tries to remove the object.

If you can see the object at the back of the throat, try to dislodge it with a sweep of your finger. Take care not to push it further down.

If the puppy faints, open its mouth and apply enough pressure at the back of the neck so that you can prevent

If an emergency should arise, you will need to be well informed so that you can take immediate action and protect the welfare of your puppy.

keeping your puppy healthy

From the moment a puppy arrives in your home, like a child, he will depend on you to provide for all his needs to keep him safe from harm.

the object from going down the throat as you hook it with your fingers.

If you cannot see the object, you will have to try to force it out from the inside. To do this, hold the puppy along your forearm with his head lowered, and strike him sharply with the heel of your hand a few times. It that doesn't work, hold the puppy with his back against you. Make a fist with one hand and place it on the abdomen above the navel. Cover the fist with your other hand, and thrust sharply upward toward the puppy's ribs. Repeat as many times as necessary.

HOW TO PERFORM ARTIFICIAL RESPIRATION

Lay the puppy on his right side on a flat, hard surface. Open the mouth, pull the tongue forward, then close the mouth again and hold it shut.

Position your head so you can see the puppy's chest, then put your mouth around the puppy's nose and blow in for about three seconds. Do not blow with a lot of force; as long as you can see the chest expand, you are blowing hard enough. Release and watch the chest fall. Repeat until the puppy breathes on his its own, or until you can turn him over to the veterinarian.

HOW TO PERFORM CPR

Lay the puppy on his right side on a flat, hard surface. If there are two people present and you can manage not to get in each other's way, have one perform artificial respiration and one massage the heart. You do this in alternating sets: one breath, six heart compression's, and repeat.

To compress the heart of a

Puppies at rest are no trouble at all, it's when they are awake that the adventure begins! Be sure to have a well-equipped first aid kit on hand in case of any mishaps.

very small puppy, grasp the puppy's chest with your thumb on one side of the sternum (the breast bone) and your fingers on the other, just behind the elbow. Obviously you can't reach the heart directly, so what you have to do to "massage" it is squeeze it between the ribs and the breast bone. Squeeze firmly six times, wait five seconds, then repeat. For larger puppies, place the heel of your hand of the side of the chest, just behind the elbow, and press down firmly. Press firmly six times, wait five seconds, then repeat. Continue until the puppy's heart beats on its own, or until you are at the emergency clinic.

FIRST-AID KIT

All dog owners will want to assemble a good first aid kit to help them in case of emergencies. Some of the basics that should be included are listed below.

- Activated charcoal
- Adhesive tape
- Antibacterial ointment (one for skin, one for eyes)
- Cardboard pieces (to cut up for splints)
- Cotton balls, cotton swabs, rolled cotton
- Anti-diarrheal medicine (intestinal protectant)
- Eyedropper or dosing syringe
- Flashlight
- Gauze pads, gauze roll
- Homeopathic remedies
- Hydrogen peroxide 3%
- Muzzle (leg of pantyhose)
- Razor blade
- Rubber gloves
- Rubbing alcohol
- Scissors
- Thermometer (baby rectal)
- Tourniquet (8-10 inch length of yarn or cloth)
- Towels and clean cloths
- Tweezers

The moment a puppy walks into your life it will never be the same. The adventures you'll have together and the love you'll share will form an unbreakable bond between you. The memories you'll have will last a lifetime.

TS-257
Choosing a Dog for Life
By Andrew De Prisco
382 pages, over 700 color
photographs.

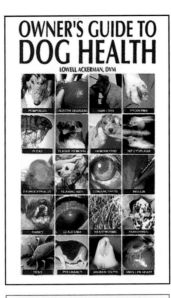

TS-214
Owner's Guide to Dog Health
By Lowell Ackerman, DVM
432 pages, over 300 color
photographs

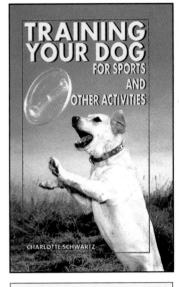

TS-258
Training Your Dog For Sports and Other Activities
By Charlotte Schwartz
160 pages, over 100 color
photographs

TS-197
The World of the Golden Retriever
By Nona Kilgore Bauer
480 pages, over 700 color
photographs

TS-293
Adopting a Great Dog: Guide to Rehoming a Rescue or Shelter Dog
By Nona Kilgore Bauer
128 pages, over 100 color
photographs

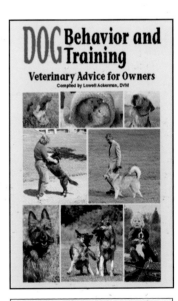

TS-252
Dog Behavior and Training: Veterinary Advice for Owners
Compiled by Dr. Lowell Ackerman
288 pages, over 200 color
photographs